W9-BNP-272

Life Before Birth

A Christian Family Book

A book for Christian families
and others
who teach the dignity of Life Before Birth

Gary E. Parker, M.S., Ed.D.

Illustrated by
Jonathan Chong
and
Lloyd R. Hight

Master
Books

Life Before Birth

First printing: July 1987
Fourth printing: April 1996

ISBN: 0-89051-164-0

Library of Congress Cataloging in Publication Data
        Parker, Gary E. 1940 -

        1. Embryology — Juvenile literature. I Chong, Jonathan, 1956 - , ill.
        2. Title

Scripture is from the King James Version.

Printed in China

Contents

Dedication

To my wife
    Mary
and our four children
    Dana Ruth
    Deborah Lynn
    David Eugene
    Diane Elizabeth

He who finds a wife finds what is good and receives favor from the Lord.

Proverbs 18:22

... Children are a heritage of the Lord: and the fruit of the womb is his reward.
Happy is the man that hath his quiver full of them ...

Psalm 127:3,5

Come, join the Parkers
as they take a wonderful
journey on the road to
LIFE BEFORE BIRTH

Chapter **1**

Knit Together

Did you ever wonder where babies come from, or what you looked like while you were growing inside your mother? Well, the Bible and biology (*by oll' oh jee*) tell us a lot about those things. The Bible tells us that each of us started as a plan in the mind of God. The tools of biology let us see how God knit us together inside our mothers.

I'm a biologist (*by oll' oh jist*)—a scientist who studies life. My children asked me how babies grow, so I took them to my lab. There I could show them pictures and models and live tadpoles to help them understand what happens.

Would you like to come along? You're welcome to join us. My name is Dr. Gary Parker, my wife is Mary, and our four children are Dana, Debbie, David, and Diane. Our adventure begins with an important question Diane asked her mother.

Mom, the new baby next door is so cute! Do you think we could have a new baby brother?

Mom: We'll see, Diane.

Where do babies come from? Sometimes I wonder how was I born.

Mom: Believe it or not, Diane, you began as a little round ball inside my body.

Really? That's how my life started—a little round ball inside of you?

Mom: That's right. Dad has a picture. Let's go ask him to show it to us.

Dad, do you have a baby picture of me before I was born?

Dad: Well, in a way I do, Diane. Let's look at page 416 in my biology book. Actually that's not you; that's another little baby. But that's the way you . looked, too, when you first started growing inside your mother.

That's it? I didn't look like much! You mean that little ball is really a baby, like me before I was born?

Dad: That's right. Besides that, this picture is over 1,000 times bigger than the baby really is when it gets started. The real you was only about the size of a dot here on this page (.)!

Mom: That special little ball you started from is called an egg cell.

Did I hatch from an egg like a chicken?

Dad: No! A chicken egg has a chicken egg cell in it. It also has a thick shell and is full of stored-up food (the yolk and the white).

Mom: You were just a single cell, Diane—with no shell. You got the food you needed from my body.

Dad: Like all cells, your egg cell was alive. That means your first cell was able to grow, react to its surroundings, and to reproduce.

Fig. 1.1 Human Egg Cell

Does my body have lots of cells, Dad?

Dad: Yes, it does. You started as just one cell. But then that one divided and grew into 2, those 2 into 4, 4 into 8, then 16 ... on up past a hundred ... a thousand ... a million ... a billion. They continued to divide until finally you had a body made up of about 50 trillion cells!

Wow! If there are that many cells, they must be very, VERY small!

Dad: They are, Diane. Your first egg cell was only the size of a dot, but that is still much bigger than the other cells. You know that microscope in my lab? Most of the time you have to look through a microscope to see a cell.

Come to think of it, Dad, how did anyone ever get the picture of an egg cell in your biology book? My egg cell was so small, and it was inside Mom, too.

Dad: Diane, doctors now have special microscopes that can look right inside the body and take pictures!

Mom: Some animal egg cells, like those of frogs and salamanders, grow outside the body. So it's easy to watch them grow in just a bowl of water.

Don't you study frogs and salamanders, Dad? Can we go to your lab and see some frog eggs and maybe watch them grow?

Dad: That's a good idea. Let's take the microscope so we can use some of the models and displays in my biology lab, too.

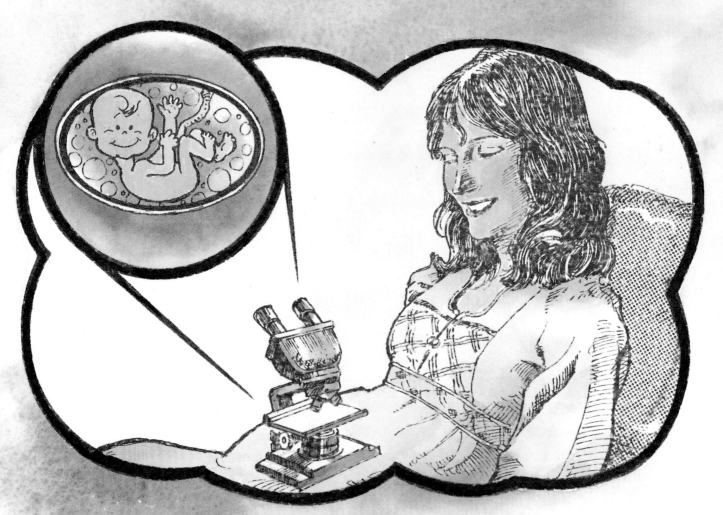

Dad: Here's a batch of frog eggs I just started last night.

Boy, frog egg cells must be a lot bigger than human egg cells!

Dad: Yes, they are. They are about ¼ inch (6 mm) across. You can watch them and work on them using just a magnifying glass or a low-power microscope.

What's that wrinkled dent in the top of this frog egg cell?

Dad: That's where the cell is dividing into two—the beginning of the frog cell's reproduction. That's what we call it when the cell begins to multiply.

Wow! That one over here looks like two cells are dividing to make four!

Dad: Good observation, Diane. That's a batch of eggs I started earlier. In this batch, you can see the tail, eyes, and mouths starting to form.

MY BABY!

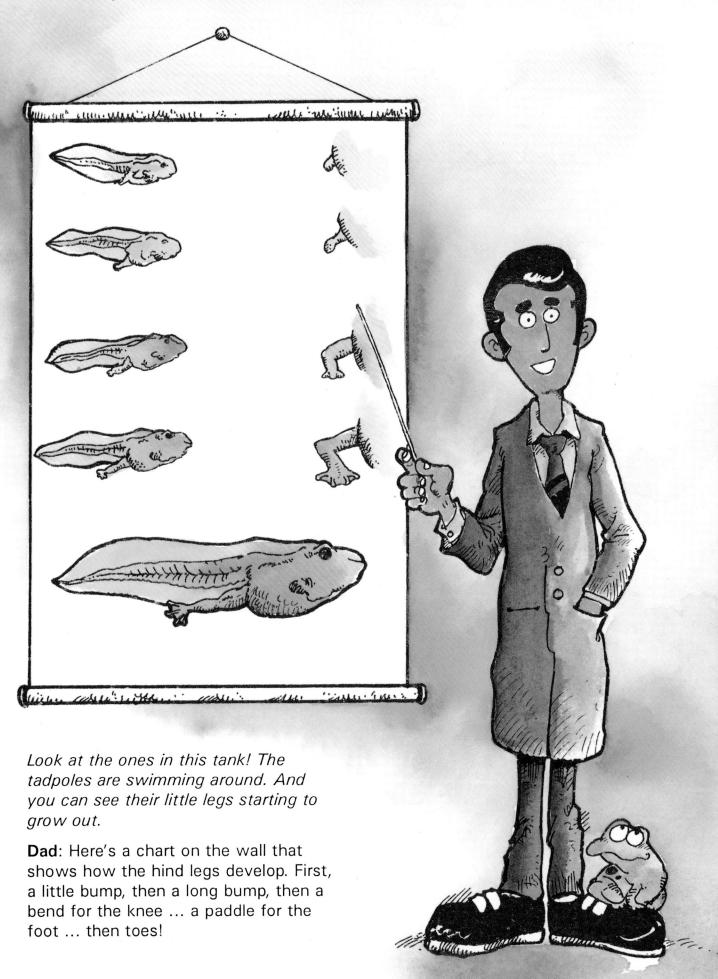

Look at the ones in this tank! The tadpoles are swimming around. And you can see their little legs starting to grow out.

Dad: Here's a chart on the wall that shows how the hind legs develop. First, a little bump, then a long bump, then a bend for the knee ... a paddle for the foot ... then toes!

I'm glad we came over to your biology lab, Dad. This place is fun! But it makes me think of a lot more questions. If I started off as just a little round ball, where did my arms and legs come from?

Dad: Diane, that's something very special. Your arms and legs, and all the rest of you, were planned ahead of time. In fact, you really began as an *idea* in the mind of *God*.

Really? Me? God was thinking about me even before I was born?

Mom: He certainly was. The Bible says — "All the days planned out for me were written in Your book before any of them came to be" (Psalm 139:16).

That was written by the shepherd boy, David, who grew up to be a king. What do you think that means, Diane?

I guess that means God planned all the days of David's life — all the things that would happen to him — even before his life began.

Dad: You see how special God thought David was.

Mom: And He thinks you're a special person, too, Diane. God also planned *your* life ahead of time, just as He did for David in the Bible.

Dad: Let's look at the egg cell again, when your life began. If we could see inside you, then we could tell ahead of time whether you would be tall or short, whether you would have brown or blonde hair. We would know if your voice would be high or low, and lots of other things.

You could? How could you tell all that?

Dad: Do you remember how you used to play with alphabet blocks?

I surely do. I thought it was fun to push the snap-ends together and line up the letters on the blocks to spell words.

Mom: You could even spell out words and leave messages with those snap-together alphabet blocks, couldn't you?

Yes. I remember one time I spelled, "Please make me a birthday cake." Then I put it in the kitchen for you to find.

Mom: I got the message!

Dad: That little egg cell, your first *living* cell, gets messages or instructions like that, too.

From alphabet blocks?

Dad: Not from alphabet blocks, of course. But a living cell gets instructions from something very special that acts a lot like those alphabet blocks.

What's that?

Dad: It's a special substance, a very long, skinny molecule, known by the initials DNA.

DNA. So that's the special stuff inside my first cell. How does DNA tell my cell what to do?

Dad: For one thing, DNA can spell out instructions just as you did with those blocks. DNA doesn't say "Please make me a birthday cake," but it does say such things to your first cell as: "Make curly hair." "Make blue eyes." "Make long fingers, a tongue that rolls up, and ear lobes that hang freely."

DNA tells your first cell what you are going to look like.

Wow! Did the DNA tell my first cell how to form ALL the parts of my body—arms and legs and eyes and ears and everything?

Mom: Not quite everything. There are many things you have to learn for yourself. And some things you have to develop with exercise, hard work, and the kind of food you eat. But all the things you inherited from your Dad and me were spelled out ahead of time in that DNA.

That's awesome! DNA is really something special! But I don't see how it can spell out so much stuff.

Dad: It's a lot like those alphabet blocks again. DNA even looks a lot like a very long string of alphabet blocks.

Do you have a picture of DNA, Dad?

Mom: Here's a model in a book your father wrote about DNA.

It DOES look like a chain of alphabet letters! What do G, C, A, and T mean?

Dad: Those are special parts of the DNA molecule. They act like letters in DNA's alphabet.

Boy, DNA has it easy. I have to learn to spell messages with 26 letters. DNA can spell messages with just four letters.

Dad: That's right, Diane—but it takes thousands of DNA letters to tell a cell how to do just one thing.

Really? DNA must be a very long string of letters!

Dad: It is. There were more than a <u>billion</u> letters in the DNA instructions in your first cell.

Wow! That's a lot!

Mom: Suppose you had to print out the instructions in your first cell on a typewriter. It would make a set of books with thousands of pages!

It's like God "typed" it on DNA. And He put all those messages inside just one little dot—my first cell. Right, Mom?

Mom: Right, Diane. God had a wonderful plan ready and waiting for you!

DNA must be very small. Could I see it with our microscope at school?

Dad: Yes and no. DNA is too thin to see by itself, unless you have a very expensive special microscope. But when the cell gets ready to reproduce, the DNA coils up tightly, like sewing thread on a spool.

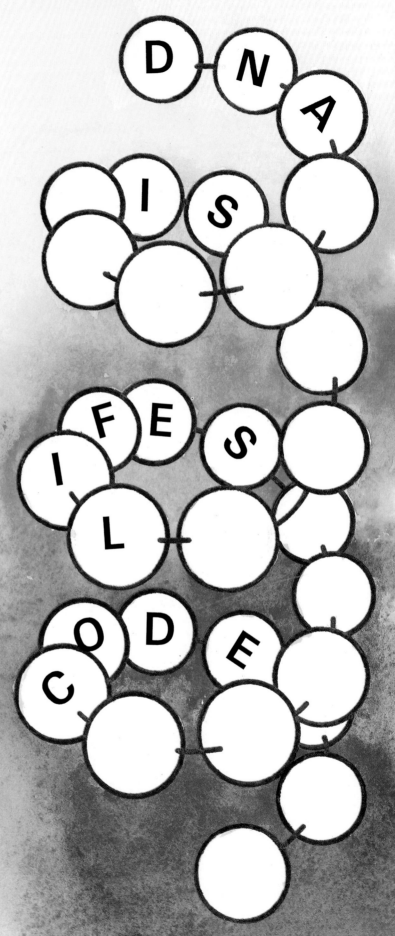

Oh, I get it. Thread is thin and hard to see. But a spool of coiled thread is thicker and easier to see.

Dad: Right you are, Diane. A thick spool of DNA all coiled up tight is

called a chromosome (*kro' moe zome*).

Mom: Here's a photograph of your father's chromosomes that your Uncle Mike made.

They look like pairs of little X's with different sizes and shapes.

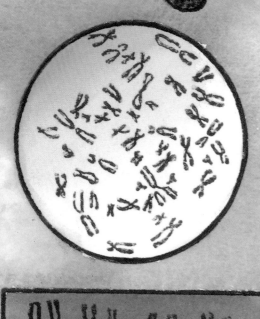

Dad: That's right. And chromosomes tell your body how to grow because they have the DNA with all those alphabet letters in them. That last pair of chromosomes is what made you a girl.

Really? You mean you could tell whether an egg cell would become a boy or girl just by looking at the chromosomes?

Dad: That's right.

Mom: Remember, God planned all of your traits ahead of time. Right from the very beginning, from your first cell, He planned for you to be a girl, and for your brother to be a boy.

Wow! When you think about all the DNA and chromosomes inside—all those plans written ahead of time—an egg cell is pretty important.

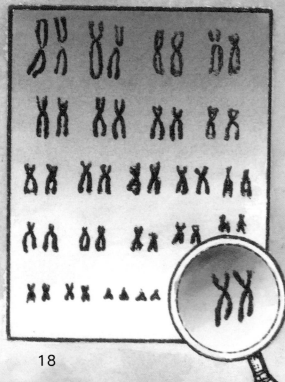

Mom: Yes, it really is.

But it surely doesn't look like much. Just a little round ball.

Dad: The Bible agrees with you.

Really!? What does the Bible say about what we looked like when our lives started?

Dad: In Psalm 139, the first part of verse 16 says God's eyes saw my "unformed body." What do you think that means?

I guess it means I didn't have any form or any shape. I was just "stuff," sort of like a lump of clay before it's molded into a special shape.

Dad: That's exactly it, Diane—and you used a good example, too. The Bible says that we are the clay, and God is the Potter (Jeremiah 18:6). God is the one who gives us our shape, like a potter can give shape to a lump of clay.

And God shapes us according to the orders He wrote out ahead of time in our DNA. Right, Dad?

Dad: Right again.

19

Mom: Here's another example, Diane. Do you remember your Great-grandmother knitting sweaters and things out of yarn?

Yes. You told me she made my baby blanket, too.

Mom: Well, a ball of yarn is sort of an "unformed substance," isn't it?

I guess so. It's just a wad of yarn without much shape.

Mom: But Great-grandma had a plan for that ball of yarn.

The plan was in my Great-grandma's mind. So I guess the ball of yarn is sort of like my "unformed body," my first cell. And the plan in Great-grandma's mind—that would be like God's plan for me written out in DNA.

Mom: That's the idea. Think about this part of verse 13 in Psalm 139. "You knit me together in my mother's womb."

"... knit me together." That sounds like God knit me together according to His plan, just as Great-grandma knit the sweater according to her plan!

20

Mom: You can't see the arms and legs in your egg cell ...

... and you can't see the arms on the sweater when it's just a ball of yarn. But the plan was already there ahead of time, just waiting to knit that "unformed" stuff together!

Dad: That's it, Diane. And the parts of the sweater appear in a certain order, too—the border, the body, and then the arms. Finally, all the parts are in place.

What about me, Dad? How was I "knit together"? What parts of me came first and second and so on?

Dad: First was your egg cell, of course.

That little round ball with the DNA plan.

Dad: Yes. Then your first cell divided many times to form a ball of many cells. Here's a picture.

Huh! You mean I looked like a blackberry or a mulberry?

Dad: Right you are. In fact, the medical name for this stage in your growth means "mulberry" (*morula*).

What happened next?

Dad: Your little mulberry absorbed food from your mother's body. It began to swell up and to form several cavities. You might call this your "hollow ball" stage.

Dad: Here's a cutaway diagram that shows what you looked like at the "hollow ball" stage.

Yikes! I surely looked funny at that stage! Do I have my own heart and blood?

Dad: At first you were so small you didn't need a heart and blood. But your heart started to pump when you were only about three weeks old. There it is in this picture, beneath your head and near the front part of your food tube.

I still didn't look like much, did I?

Head

Heart

Food tube

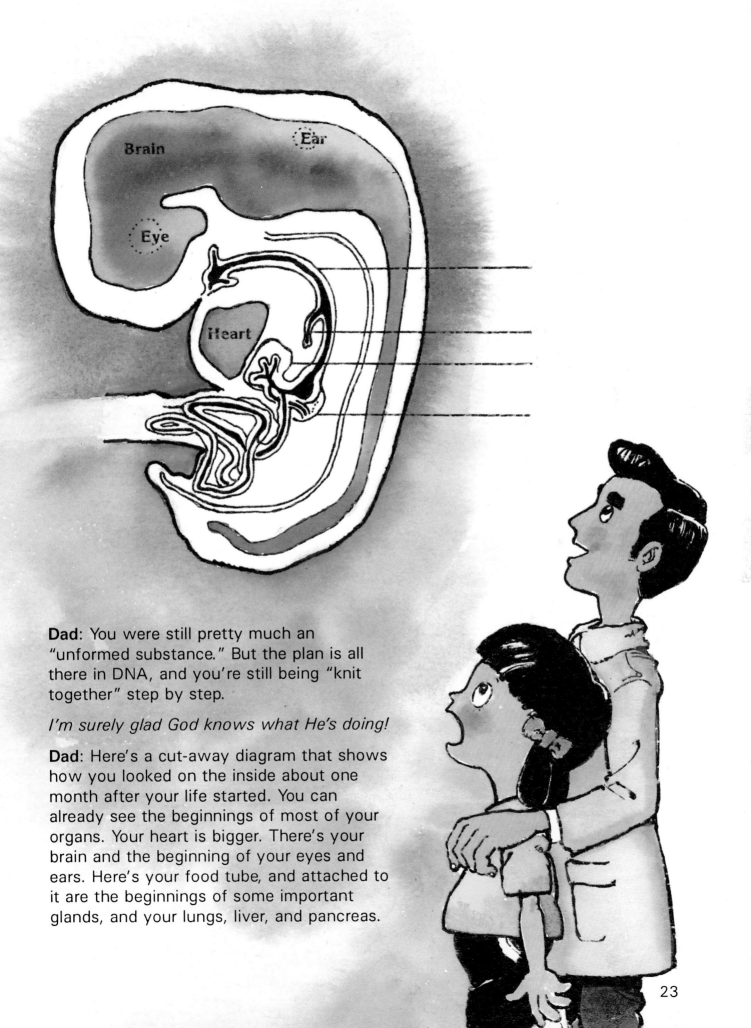

Brain

Ear

Eye

Heart

Dad: You were still pretty much an "unformed substance." But the plan is all there in DNA, and you're still being "knit together" step by step.

I'm surely glad God knows what He's doing!

Dad: Here's a cut-away diagram that shows how you looked on the inside about one month after your life started. You can already see the beginnings of most of your organs. Your heart is bigger. There's your brain and the beginning of your eyes and ears. Here's your food tube, and attached to it are the beginnings of some important glands, and your lungs, liver, and pancreas.

Mom: Here's what you looked like on the outside about one month after your egg cell started to grow, Diane.

Now that's more like it! I can see my face, and my arms and legs have started to form! But what's that rope attached to my belly button?

Mom: That "rope" is your "life line." It's the umbilical (*um bil' i kul*) cord, just called "cord" for short. It's sort of like an air hose for a deep sea diver, or the hoses to an astronaut in space. You pumped blood out toward my body through that cord. My body picked up wastes from your blood, and sent food and oxygen back through the cord to you.

Thanks, Mom! What happens to the cord when we're born?

Mom: Usually the doctor ties it off and cuts it. Then it shrivels up. It would shut itself off and shrivel up even without the doctor's help, though. There's a little scar on your body where you were once attached to my body.

How big am I now?

Dad: You are only about *one inch* (25 mm) long, and weigh less than *one ounce* (28 g). When you were that size, you could fit easily in the palm of my hand!

Wow! But even that small, you can tell just by looking at me that I'm a person.

Mom: You were YOU, a special person, even as an egg cell. But you're right—now you can begin to see God's plan in DNA take shape.

Dad: By two months after your life began, you had little fingers and toes, even though it was still seven months before you would be born.

Mom: You were even able to swim around in your special "bag of waters." And, before long, I could feel you kick.

Dad: Your body has many different kinds of cells in it. Your egg cell was just sort of round and blah. But some cells it produced became long and wiry nerve cells, tough and fiber-like muscle cells, pancake-shaped skin cells, and so on.

25

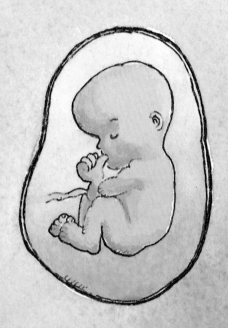

Mom: Here you are at the "halfway" point—4½ months after your life began, and 4½ months before you left my body to be born.

Dad: You weighed only a little more than a pound (0.5 kg), but all your major organs were formed. Your brain was "making waves." You kicked. You even sucked your thumb! If you had been born very early or "premature," you could even have lived outside your mother's body at this stage. But you would have needed lots of special care.

I guess God was really taking special care of me all along.

Mom: Another verse in Psalm 139 tells the story of David's life, and ours, too.

What verse is that, Mother?

Mom: "I praise you, for I am fearfully and wonderfully made" (Psalm 139:14).

Dad: "Fearfully and wonderfully made." A perfect summary! And reason indeed to praise our great and gracious God!

27

Chapter 2

No Useless Leftovers!

Each of us started life as a unique person, planned ahead of time by God, and knit together inside our mother's womb. But some people wonder if we are really human beings before we are born. Some even believe that our bodies have the leftover parts of animals inside them.

Were we people before we were born? Do we have useless leftover animal parts inside us? The Bible and biology seem to agree: *Yes*, we were people inside our mothers; and *No*, we do not have leftover animal parts inside us. Our oldest daughter, Dana, asked me why I said that. Let's find out together.

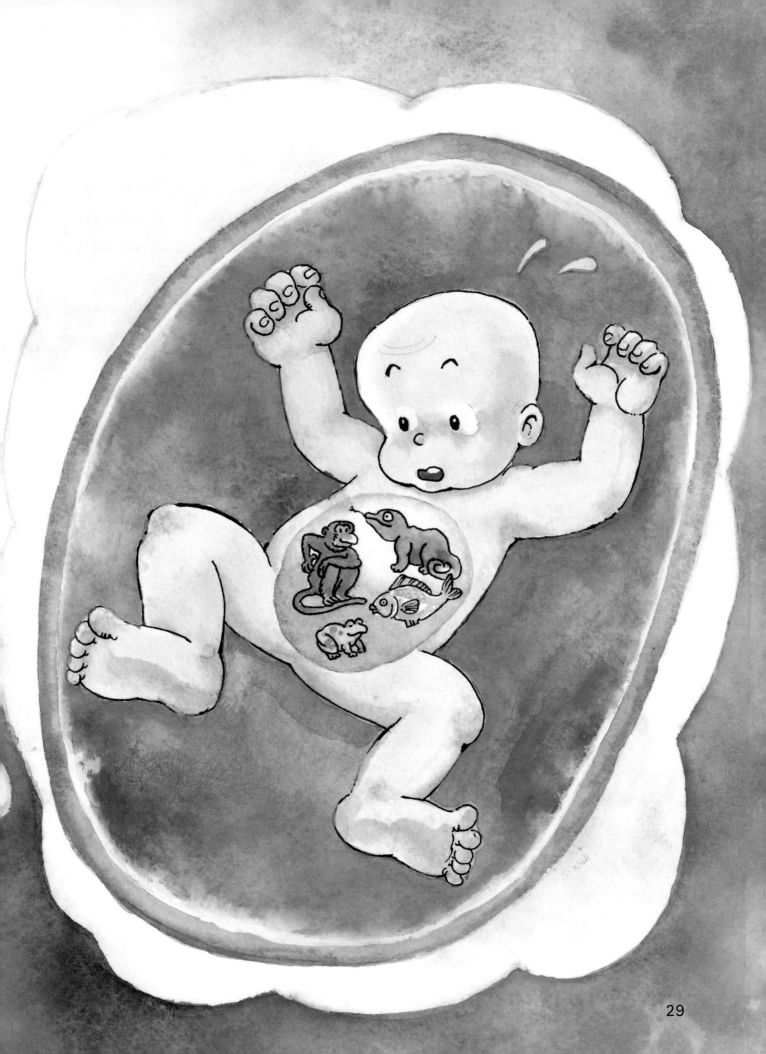

Dad, is this the picture you showed Diane—the one that shows what she looked like about a month after her life began?

Dad: Yes it is.

Did you tell Diane that she was a human being, a little person, when she looked like this?

Dad: Of course. And so were you at that stage of your life. *After* you are born, you go through stages when you are called a baby, infant, toddler, teen, and finally adult. **Before** you are born, you go through stages when you are called an egg cell, embryo (*em' bree o*), and fetus (*feet' us*). That picture shows what you and Diane looked like at the *embryo* stage.

Embryo. So even when we were tiny embryos, Diane and I were real people—human beings. Right, Dad?

Dad: Yes you were, Dana. Your arms and legs, eyes and ears, brain and heart, liver and lungs were already developing. Your chromosomes were all set to make you a girl. If we could read God's plan in your DNA, we could tell, even at this stage, whether you would be tall or short, have light or dark hair. We could tell if you would talk and sing with a high or low voice, and lots of other things. You were already our special daughter. Remember that when you sing "God made me special; I'm the only one of my kind."

Thanks, Dad. I'm glad to hear that.

31

Dad: Why? You seem to have a special reason for asking all those questions.

I did. I showed that embryo picture to one of my friends from school.

Dad: And?

And he said the picture showed the opposite of what you just said. He said the picture showed God did NOT create us as human beings, at least not from the beginning.

Dad: Oh? I think I know why he said that. But you tell me.

He showed me three things on the embryo that he said were not human.

Dad: I thought so. Do you remember what he showed you?

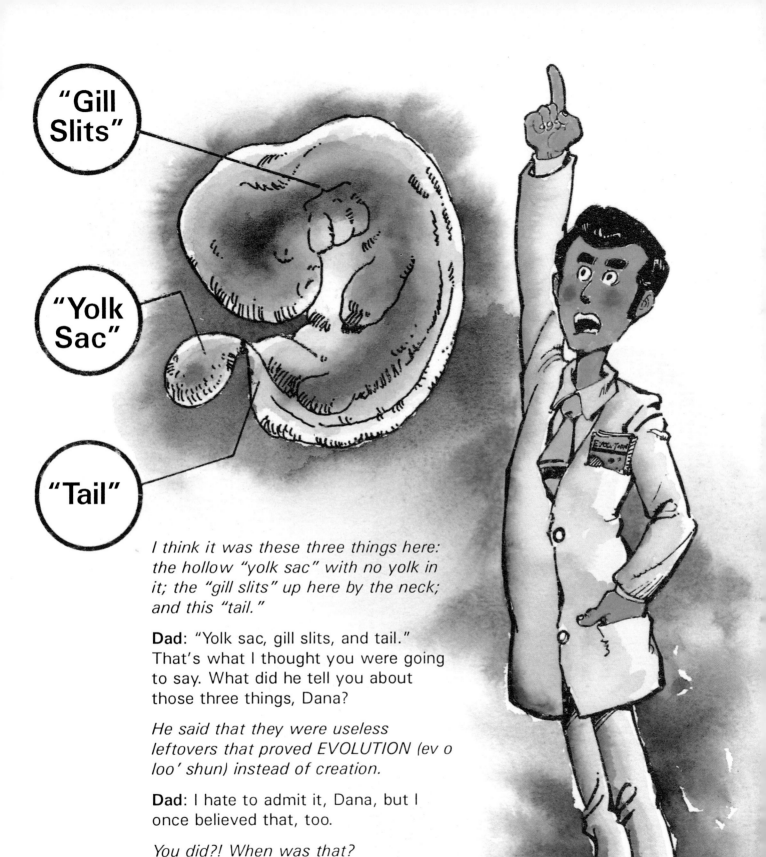

"Gill Slits"

"Yolk Sac"

"Tail"

I think it was these three things here: the hollow "yolk sac" with no yolk in it; the "gill slits" up here by the neck; and this "tail."

Dad: "Yolk sac, gill slits, and tail." That's what I thought you were going to say. What did he tell you about those three things, Dana?

He said that they were useless leftovers that proved EVOLUTION (ev o loo' shun) instead of creation.

Dad: I hate to admit it, Dana, but I once believed that, too.

You did?! When was that?

Dad: When I first started teaching college biology, Dana, I believed in evolution. It was all I had been taught. I taught my students evolution, too, instead of creation.

What exactly is "evolution" anyway, Dad? What makes evolution different from creation?

Dad: Well, the Bible tells us we each began as a plan in the mind of God. He is our Creator. God took the dust of the ground and shaped it into the body of the first man, Adam, who was a real person. Think about how a master sculptor carves a magnificent statue from a block of marble. Or imagine an engineer who could make a walking, talking robot. The works of an artist or an engineer tell us something about the way God created. But God is much more than man. He could breathe *life* into what He made.

Well, Mom told me that creation begins with plan and purpose, and works toward a goal. What about evolution? How does evolution begin?

Dad: According to evolution, people *did* start as dust, or "dead" stuff, but it was *not* shaped by God. There was no purpose, no planning ahead, no goal. Instead, by comparison, it was something like a desert wind gradually shaping a rock that made life. Furthermore, they say the first life looked like a cell, then a fish, a reptile, an ape, and finally a human being. Time and chance, "a lucky roll of the dice," replaces the plan and purpose of God. But it's very hard for many scientists—even those who accept evolution—to believe that time and chance could bring "dead" stuff to life.

I know you collect rocks and arrowheads, Dad. It sounds to me like the difference between creation and evolution is like the difference between an ARROWHEAD carved with PLAN AND PURPOSE and a tumbled PEBBLE shaped by TIME AND CHANCE. That's a BIG difference!

Dad: That's a good, clear, simple example, too, Dana.

But what about those useless leftovers—the yolk sac, gill slits, and tail?

Dad: When I taught evolution, I told my students that gill slits in the embryo were useless leftovers of the fish stage in human evolution. The empty yolk sac was a useless leftover of the lizard or reptile stage. And the tail told us that our ancestors—the apes and monkeys—swung down from the trees.

That sounds weird, Dad. But if the yolk sac has no yolk in it, what purpose could it have?

Dad: It has no yolk in it because it is not for the purpose of feeding the little embryo. You got your food from your mother's bloodstream.

ARROW HEADS FROM ARIZONA

rocks

Is the yolk sac a useless leftover, then?

Dad: Not at all! It makes the first blood cells. That blood is needed to make the bone that later takes over the job of making blood cells for you. So, the so-called "yolk sac" is really a "blood-forming sac," and it's absolutely necessary for *human* life.

Then it's not a useless leftover of evolution! Why would anyone ever call the human embryo's blood-forming sac a "yolk sac"?

Dad: Back in the 1800's, belief in evolution was very strong among certain people, and some had a strong desire to stamp out the very idea of creation. One such person, a scientist named Haeckel, even changed his diagrams of embryos to make them look more like stages in evolution!

Did he get caught?

Dad: Yes, he did—by scientists more dedicated to the truth than to evolution!

What did he say about the diagrams he changed?

Dad: He tried to excuse himself by saying that others changed their diagrams to make them favor evolution, too.

That's awful, Dad. That's not the way science is supposed to work!

Dad: You're right there, Dana. In fact, the whole idea of the human body filled with useless leftovers of evolution was very bad for science.

What do you mean, Dad?

Dad: You've seen how big your brother's tonsils are, haven't you?

Yes. So?

Dad: Well, people who believe in evolution once thought that tonsils were useless leftovers of evolution. That was back when your Grandfather was just starting out as a medical doctor, a surgeon.

If doctors thought that tonsils were useless leftovers, did they just leave them alone?

Dad: Even worse, Dana. Of course, not all doctors believed they were useless leftovers of evolution, but some who did would actually take healthy tonsils out of healthy children.

Really? Why would anyone do that?

Dad: That's just one case where widespread belief in evolution led to "medical malpractice." Of course the doctors thought they were helping the child by removing a useless organ that might get diseased. In reality, they were doing just the opposite. Tonsils are important organs for *fighting* disease.

I guess that news comes too late for a lot of people, huh, Dad?

Dad: I'm afraid so, Dana.

But what about tonsils that DO get diseased? One of my friends at school was always getting a sore throat. She just had her tonsils taken out.

Dad: That's a different story. Any organ in the body can be damaged by disease, and some have to be taken out. Doctors take out stomachs, kidneys, and intestines when they get badly diseased. That doesn't mean they are useless leftovers of evolution!

Come to think of it, doctors can even replace hearts, lungs, and livers that get diseased. They surely aren't useless leftovers!

I can see another reason the idea of useless leftovers would be very bad for science. If you believe an organ has no use, you don't bother to study it.

Dad: Good point, Dana. Evolution believers in the 1800's listed 180 "useless leftovers" of evolution in the human body. Now we have discovered the proper functions for **all of them**. But it took longer than it should have. The evolution idea of useless leftovers held back the progress of science for over 100 years in many cases.

How did the idea of useless leftovers ever get started, anyway?

Dad: It didn't start with science, that's for sure. It really started with the desire to prove that God does not exist, or at least that "God" is a bad designer.

Really? What do you mean, Dad?

Dad: I got the idea from a scientist in Canada who was studying the history of science. He showed that the early believers in evolution did not even try to prove that organs had no function. They just assumed it. Then they tried to say that organs with no functions proved "God" didn't know what He was doing.

And really it was the evolution believers who didn't know what they were doing!

Dad: That's about it, Dana.

What evolution believers thought was BAD design was really evidence of GOOD design.

Dad: Oh? What do you mean?

Take that so-called yolk-sac, for instance. It is outside the body. So, God could use it to make the first blood cells, then just let it shrivel up when its job was done. It wouldn't get in the way of other organs.

Dad: Hey, that's a good thought! Besides that, God could use the same structure in other life forms for both blood cells *and* yolk, if a yolk was needed.

Now that sounds like GOOD design to me—getting many uses out of the same part. To me, that's like human designers using steel I-beams. They can use them to make tall buildings, long bridges, mobile home frames, and lots of other things.

Dad: Good example. Using the same structure for different uses *is* good engineering design. Sounds like you'd make a good design engineer.

41

Thanks, Dad. Whoops ... I just thought of something. What about those gill slits and tail? How could gill slits and a tail be good design for a human embryo?

Dad: First of all, Dana, those are the wrong labels again. The human embryo has *never* had gills or slits, so it's certainly wrong to name them gill slits!

But Dad, there are little dents or grooves in the skin in this picture of the human embryo. If those aren't gill slits, what are they?

Dad: They are pouches and grooves near the throat or pharynx (*fair' inks*). They are called pharyngeal (*fair rinj' geal*) pouches, but we can call them throat pouches.

What do they do?

Dad: In fish, the pouches and grooves grow together to make a series of gill slits. The fish takes in water through its mouth. Then it squeezes the water out through the gill slits while the gills absorb oxygen.

Does the human embryo do that?

HI, MOM!

42

Dad: No. You get your oxygen "piped in" from your mother. Your umbilical cord picks it up for you from her bloodstream, like an air hose to a deep sea diver (except the oxygen is dissolved in the blood).

Why did I have gill slits as an embryo, then?

Dad: You didn't. Remember? You had **throat pouches**, not gill slits.

Oh, yes. Did these throat pouches just come and go, or did they do something for me?

Dad: Those throat pouches were absolutely necessary for your development as a person.

Really? What did they do?

Dad: Those pouches became germ-fighting organs, your two middle ear canals, and two important glands.

What glands?

Dad: The parathyroid and thymus glands. The parathyroid (*pair ah thigh' roid*) glands help to regulate your calcium; you'd die quickly without them. Without the thymus (*thigh' muss*) gland, you would be unable to survive in a world full of germs; you need it to start up "half" your disease-fighting system.

I know one thing for sure, those throat pouches aren't useless leftovers of evolution! Another thing, they aren't gill slits, either!

Dad: You're right both times, Dana.

But what about the so-called "tail"? Does it show creation instead of evolution?

Dad: Yes, it certainly does, Dana. As an embryo, you never had a "yolk sac," you never had "gill slits," …

And I'll bet I never had a "tail," either.

Dad: Right. The end of your spine stuck out, as it does in this picture, simply because it developed faster than the leg and "rear end" muscles around it. As those muscles developed, the end of your spine wound up inside as a hook of bone called the coccyx (*kok' six*)—also falsely called the "tail bone."

Does it ever wiggle or act like a tail?

Dad: Never. Instead it forms a place for muscles to attach. These muscles help to give us a very special *human* ability, the ability to stand upright, and to sit the way we do.

44

Then, instead of calling it the "tail bone," maybe we should call it the "posture bone."

Dad: Good idea, Dana. There's a way you can prove how important the "posture bone" is for human beings, too—but I don't recommend it.

What's that, Dad?

Dad: Fall down the stairs and land on your so-called "tail bone"—that "posture bone."

I had a friend who did that. He could hardly stand up, sit down, or even lie down. About all he could do for two weeks was moan and groan!

Dad: He learned the hard way how important the end of the spine is for human posture. It also supports some muscles that work with the lower end of your intestines. Let's just say you'd have trouble going to the bathroom if that bone wasn't working right!

Never mind the details, Dad. I get the picture. The end of the spine is NOT a useless leftover of evolution. Instead, it is something we need as part of our design as human beings!

45

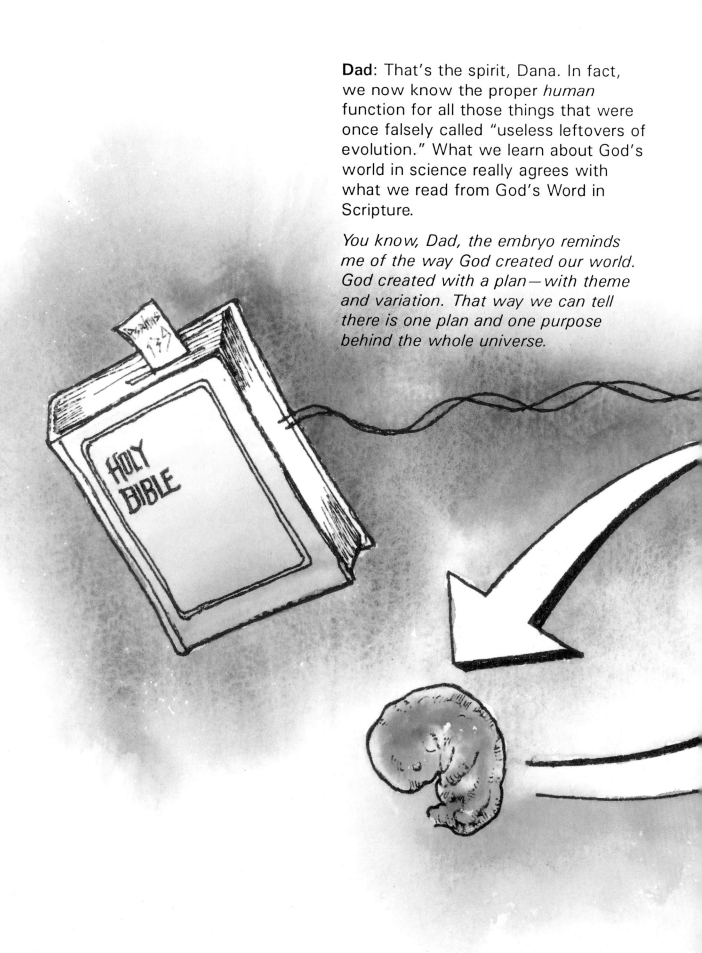

Dad: That's the spirit, Dana. In fact, we now know the proper *human* function for all those things that were once falsely called "useless leftovers of evolution." What we learn about God's world in science really agrees with what we read from God's Word in Scripture.

You know, Dad, the embryo reminds me of the way God created our world. God created with a plan—with theme and variation. That way we can tell there is one plan and one purpose behind the whole universe.

Dad: I like that idea, Dana. Even as an embryo, you were a human being. That's God's theme. But you were also my own special daughter—***God's special creation***.

I guess the best summary is still there in Psalm 139. God planned my life before I was born. Then He took my "unformed substance"— my first cell—and "knit me together" inside Mom. Like each and every other person, I am "fearfully and wonderfully made."

Dad: Amen, Dana. Praise God!

Chapter 3

Planned by God

It's a miracle—the way a little human being develops inside his or her mother. All the parts have to form at the right time in the right order at the right place. It's fun to tell people about the way we were each "knit together" according to God's special plan. In fact, that's one way to tell people about Christ, our Creator, Savior, and Lord.

But you had better be ready for some tough questions, too. People who believe in evolution try to use certain things about life before birth to argue against creation. The Apostle Peter tells us (1 Peter 3:15): "Be ready always to give a reason for the hope that is within you, yet in gentleness and meekness." We need a mind full of knowledge and a heart full of love to witness to the truth of God's Word through the things in His world.

Our daughter, Debbie, had a chance to put those Biblical principles into practice.

Dad, do you remember that stuff about a "human tail" you told Dana?

Dad: Yes.

You said the human embryo never really has a tail, didn't you? You said it was just the end of the spine that stuck out. It developed into important things we need as human beings. Is that right?

Dad: That's right.

Well, I told my friend what you said. He told his teacher, and his teacher said that you are wrong.

Dad: Oh? Why is that?

Well, the teacher read a newspaper article to the whole class. According to the news story, there was a baby born with a tail. There was a doctor who told about it. He said the baby's tail showed evolution. It showed that before people were people, we were just animals, like monkeys, that swung by their tails from the trees!

Dad: I remember reading that story myself. It was even written up in a popular magazine for doctors.

Well, is it true? Was there a baby born with a tail?

Dad: Yes and no.

Yes and no? What kind of answer is that?

Dad: "Yes" it is true that a doctor wrote such an article claiming a baby was born with a tail. But "no" it is *not* true at all that the baby was actually born with a tail.

Wait a minute. If the baby didn't have a tail, why did the doctor say he did?

Dad: The baby did have a little flap of skin near the end of his spine. It looked sort of like a tiny finger. It was about ¼ inch across, 2 inches long, and ½ inch off the center of the backbone.

Did the little flap have part of the backbone in it, and the nerve cord? Did it have muscles so it could wiggle?

Dad: No, Debbie, it had none of those things. No bone, no spinal nerve cord, no tail-wagging muscles. It was nothing more than skin and a little fat.

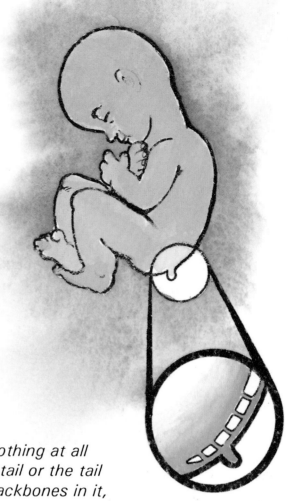

That's not a tail! That's nothing at all like a cat's tail or a dog's tail or the tail of a monkey! A tail has backbones in it, and part of the nerve cord, and big muscles!

Dad: I wish that doctor knew as much about what it takes to make a tail as you do!

It was just skin and fat. It was even off-center. That makes me mad. Why in the world would a doctor call an off-center flap of skin and fat a tail?

Dad: That's a very good question. At first I thought it was just a joke, maybe even something to test how easy it is to fool news people with fake science. But it was even written up in a popular medical magazine.

You mean he was serious?

Dad: Yes, he was. I guess in a way that tale of a tail shows how evolution can make a person blind to the simple facts of science.

The doctor wanted very badly to believe that human beings came from animals with tails. So he jumped at the chance to call that flap of skin and fat a tail. He wasn't very careful with his science.

Dad: Today, "everybody who's anybody" is supposed to believe in evolution—or so we're told. So, believers in evolution get away with some really non-scientific nonsense!

That "tail" sounds like a great example of "non-science" and "non-sense."

Dad: Think of the effect that error in evolution might have had on the mother, too.

What do you mean?

Dad: If the mother found out, she might think, "Oh, no. I've given birth to a 'throwback' to the monkey stage!" You can almost hear the husband and wife start arguing. "Your side of the family is to blame!" "No, it's yours!" Enough people believe in evolution today that hospitals usually don't like to tell a mother something that might make her think her baby is a "throwback" to some animal stage in evolution.

All that, and the baby didn't really have a tail at all! What happened to the baby, anyway?

Dad: Nothing. A doctor just snipped off the little flap of skin and fat. It was a very easy job. He didn't have to cut through a bone, or the spinal nerve cord, or even any large blood vessels.

That sounds much easier than cutting off a real tail from a cat or dog, like a vet does for dobermans.

Dad: It was much easier—more like removing a wart than amputating a real tail!

Do you know of other examples like that, Dad?

Dad: Yes, there are several. Sometimes a child is born with a hole in his or her neck, and …

… and I'll bet some evolution believers say that's like a gill slit, a "throwback" to the fish stage.

Dad: You're right! But, of course, it isn't. The hole in the baby's neck has no flaps full of blood vessels to absorb oxygen from water! It's no gill at all, and it's quite easily repaired.

The hole really tells us about how the baby grows, not about how evolution happened.

Dad: Right, Deb. Now here's a mistake in the embryo that evolution believers never use. Sometimes a baby is born with an upper lip or roof of the mouth that don't quite meet in the middle. (Those conditions are called "hare lip" and "cleft palate.")

I guess no evolution believer would ever use that to prove we evolved from animals with a break in the upper lip or roof of the mouth!

Dad: No, because those mistakes teach us nothing about evolution. But they do teach us about the way the little baby grows. Believe it or not, Debbie, your pretty face formed by parts growing in from your right and left sides, but sometimes they don't grow far enough.

That must be why there's a gap in the middle.

Dad: That's it exactly. Doctors can repair the mistake, although sometimes it's a tough job.

I guess evolution doesn't really help scientists learn anything about the way a baby develops inside his or her mother.

Dad: It gets even worse than that. Evolution has given us some very false and harmful ideas about how babies develop.

You mean like making us think tonsils were useless leftovers of evolution?

Dad: Even worse.

You mean like maybe making a mother think her child was a "throwback" to the monkey stage of evolution because he was born with a flap of skin near the end of the spine?

Dad: Yes. I think that the "throwback" idea is probably the worst idea in evolution. Have you ever heard of something called "Mongoloid idiocy"?

53

Yes. We learned about it in school. Only our teacher said you aren't supposed to call it Mongoloid idiocy. He said it's supposed to be called Down's something.

Dad: Down's syndrome. Dr. Down was a doctor in England in the late 1800's. He was the first to describe the set of features (or syndrome) certain babies had in common.

I know two people at school who were Down's babies. They are both so nice. I think they are in the slow learner's class, but I'm not sure. What causes Down's anyway?

Dad: It's "too much of a good thing," Debbie. Down's babies started with one extra chromosome in their first cell. Do you remember what a chromosome is?

Yes. A chromosome is like a spool of DNA, the molecule that tells our bodies how to grow.

Dad: That's right. Most people are born with 46 chromosomes in each cell, 23 pairs. But the babies with Down's syndrome are born with 47 chromosomes in each cell.

What happens because of that extra chromosome, Daddy?

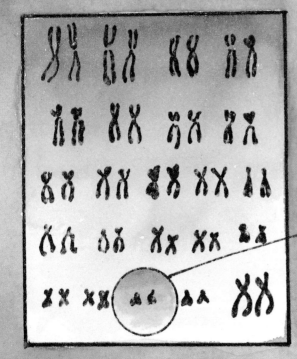

Dad: The results vary quite a bit. Sometimes there are a lot of mental and physical handicaps, sometimes only one or the other. Sometimes there's very little effect. Often a Down's child can grow up to go to school and work in their adult life.

Why did Dr. Down call that extra chromosome condition "Mongoloid idiocy"?

Dad: Back in the 1800's, Dr. Down didn't know about that chromosome. But he had observed that these children had faces and eyes with an Oriental shape, even though their parents were English. That's why he called it "Mongoloid." But here's the sad part. He called the condition "idiocy" because he thought these children were "throwbacks" to the "Mongoloid stage" of evolution. Even worse, he thought Mongoloids had evolved only to the idiot level of intelligence.

That's insulting to the Orientals, isn't it? How could anybody ever believe anything like that? Orientals were civilized people in the 1800's. In fact, their civilization goes back further than the European civilization where Dr. Down lived!

Dad: You're absolutely right. It's like that doctor who tried to call a flap of skin and fat a tail. It's obviously non-scientific nonsense. It's utterly at odds with everything we know now—and knew then!

Maybe it's like you said before. Dr. Down's belief in evolution was so strong, it just blinded him to the plain and simple facts—the facts of Scripture as well as the facts of science.

Dad: I think you're probably right. Even worse, Dr. Down was not alone. Many people who should have known better went along with him. Even into the 1920's and 1930's many scientists who believed in evolution thought that the native peoples of Africa and Australia were just leftovers from stages in evolution, not yet fully human.

That's awful! I'm glad nobody believes in that kind of evolution anymore.

Mom: I hate to tell you this, Deb, but things may be worse now, not better. Today there are people all over the world who think it is perfectly okay to take the life of a baby before it is born.

You mean abortion (ah bore' shun)?

Dad: That's right.

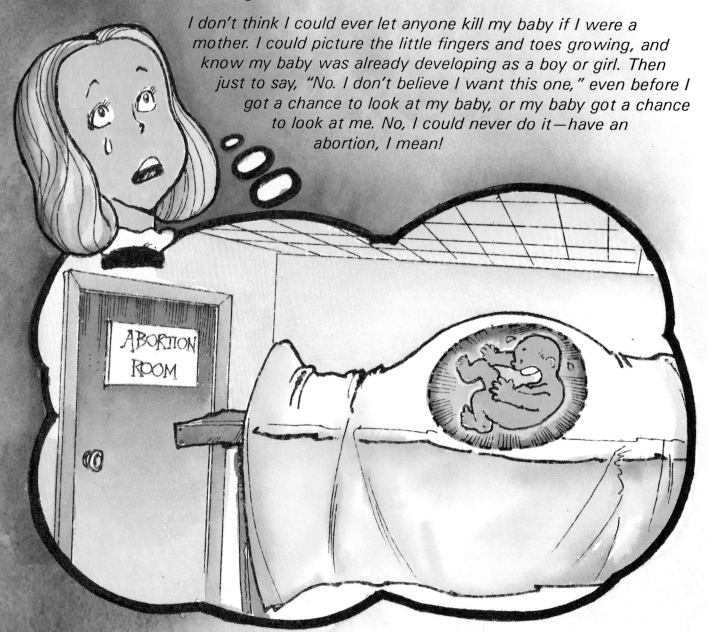

I don't think I could ever let anyone kill my baby if I were a mother. I could picture the little fingers and toes growing, and know my baby was already developing as a boy or girl. Then just to say, "No. I don't believe I want this one," even before I got a chance to look at my baby, or my baby got a chance to look at me. No, I could never do it—have an abortion, I mean!

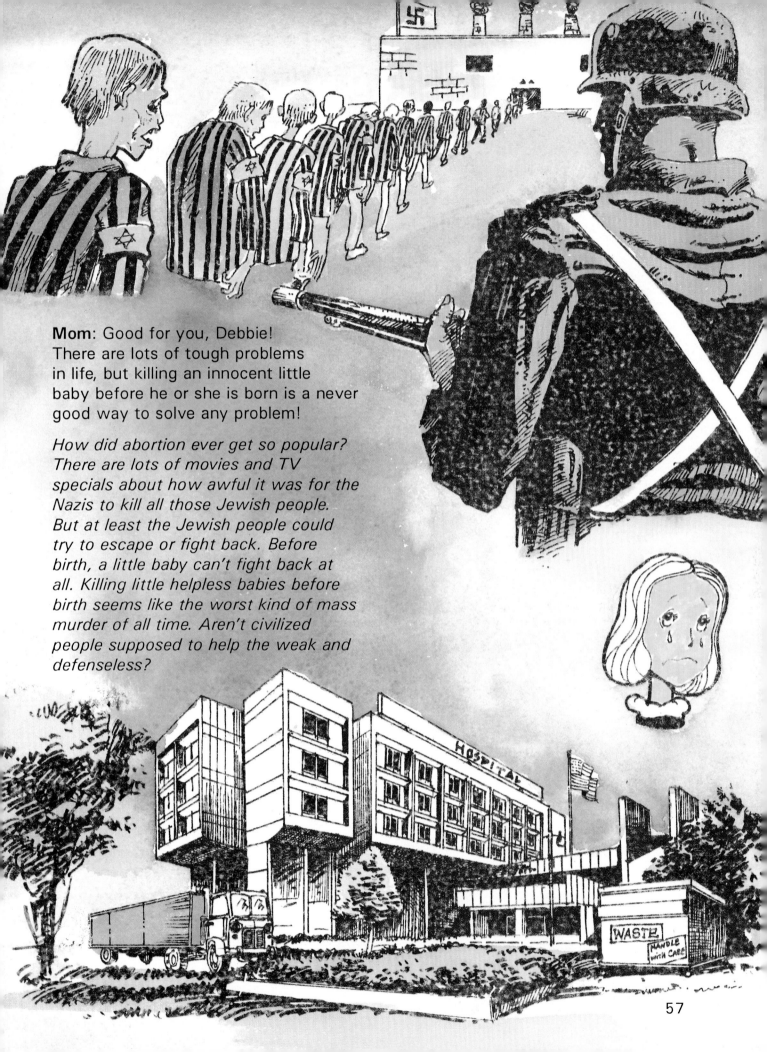

Mom: Good for you, Debbie! There are lots of tough problems in life, but killing an innocent little baby before he or she is born is a never good way to solve any problem!

How did abortion ever get so popular? There are lots of movies and TV specials about how awful it was for the Nazis to kill all those Jewish people. But at least the Jewish people could try to escape or fight back. Before birth, a little baby can't fight back at all. Killing little helpless babies before birth seems like the worst kind of mass murder of all time. Aren't civilized people supposed to help the weak and defenseless?

57

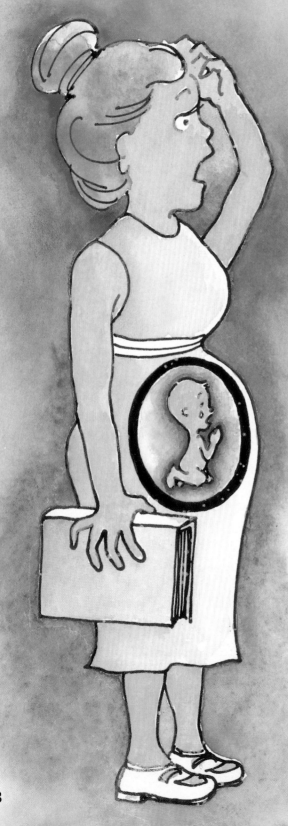

Dad: You would think so, Debbie. But in our country, it's the laws and the courts—even the Supreme Court—that say it's okay for a mother to let someone take the life of her unborn child.

I don't see how people who would kill a baby, or help other people kill babies, could ever go to heaven.

Dad: Wait a minute, Deb. Remember, everyone, you and I included, has done things that separate us from the love of God. "All have sinned" (Romans 3:23). But, thanks to God for His grace and forgiveness in Jesus Christ, anyone can be saved! As Jesus said, whoever is sorry for his or her sins and repents—turns away from sin and toward God—He will in no way cast out (John 6:37).

God with His grace and love will take care of the babies that have been aborted, too.

You're right, Daddy. But is there anything we can do to help stop abortion?

Dad: It would really help if people knew that a baby before birth is a living, special, tiny, individual human being, *not* just a part of the mother's body, and certainly *not* some animal or stage of evolution!

Maybe before any mother can have an abortion, she should see pictures of what her baby looks like. She should be told how the baby is already swimming and kicking and even thumb-sucking. The precious little feet and hands with the tiny fingers and toes are so cute, too.

Mom: We can all help by supporting right-to-life groups, and voting for officials and judges who respect life—everyone's life.

Dad: Your Mom is right, but I think we must go even further than that. It's hard to pass correct laws if your heart and mind are not correct. People really need to see that *each life* is a special gift from God, and, even if imperfect in our eyes, each person is a perfect part of His total plan.

I agree, Dad. But I heard someone say, "Every baby should be wanted and unwanted babies shouldn't be born."

60

Dad: I'm sorry to say I've heard that too. Many people don't want to admit that God is the creator and giver of life. Only He has the *right* to say who should live or die (Deuteronomy 32:38; I Samuel 2:6). And, just as soon as the egg cell begins to grow, that tiny, tiny baby is already a living human being.

Mom: One thing for sure: adoption is better than abortion.

But, wouldn't it be hard to give your baby away?

Mom: Yes, it would, Debbie. But adoption is an act of love, and the parents know that in this way the baby will be getting something better than they can provide.

Dad: There are many married couples who can't have children and are praying to adopt a baby. They would love the baby and raise it as their very own.

Mom: Little ones are very precious to God. Jesus loved to have little children around Him (Mark 10:16). He commanded us to love and care for *each one*. He says in Matthew 18:10 that we are *not to despise* one of these little ones.

It's hard to understand how they could have disobeyed God and made a law that allowed abortion.

Dad: Yes, I know, Debbie. But, I think the "throwback theory" of evolution had something to do with it.

The "throwback theory." Is that what we've been talking about?

Dad: Yes. It's the idea that a human being goes through so-called stages of evolution as "it" develops inside "its" mother.

You mean that the "gill slits" are supposed to be the fish stage, the "yolk sac" the lizard stage, and the "tail" the monkey stage?

Dad: I'm afraid so. In fact, your very first cell—the egg cell—was once called the "amoeba stage" in evolution.

*Amoeba (**ah me' bah**). That's a little one-celled animal, isn't it?*

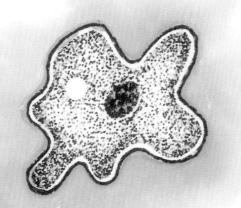

62

Dad: Yes, and it is true that you were once the same size as an amoeba. When you were an egg cell, you were almost exactly the same size and shape as a mouse cell, elephant cell, and certain one-celled animals. Does that "prove" you must be related to them?

Don't be silly Dad. That's just how it LOOKS on the outside. If you look at just the outside shape, you could say I evolved from a marble, a bee-bee, or a ball bearing—they're small, round things, too!

Dad: Very good, Deb, and that's a clever way to put it, too!

If you look INSIDE an amoeba, or inside the egg cell of a man, mouse, or elephant—or inside a marble—all those things are totally different.

Dad: Right again, Debbie. When it comes to the DNA plan inside your egg cell, you were just as different from a mouse or an elephant then as you are now. In fact, you were a human being—a very special, individual person—right from your first cell!

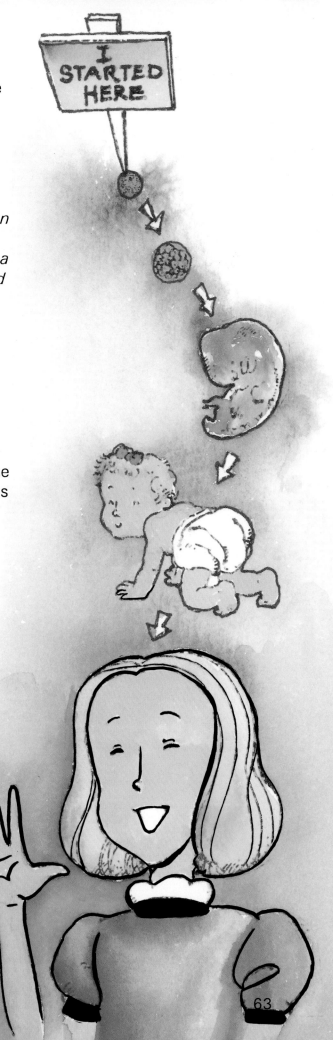

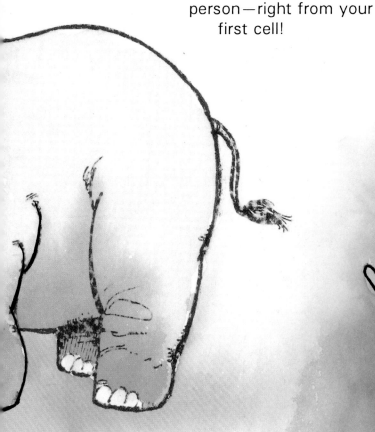

63

Why would anybody believe in the "throwback theory" of evolution?

Dad: Actually, scientists who have studied the human embryo do *not* believe that anymore. I once debated a college professor in Canada. Although he believed in evolution, he said evolution scientists quit believing in the throwback theory over 40 years ago!

It seems to me, the MORE people really know about science, the LESS likely they are to believe that life before birth shows evolution.

Dad: That's an excellent observation, Debbie.

You know, Dad, I was just thinking. Human life before birth doesn't show stages of evolution. It really shows the stages of creation instead.

Dad: Oh? Tell me why you think so.

Well, it's like what Diane read from Psalm 139. We start off with God's plan "written" in our DNA code. At first, we are each just an "unformed substance"—the egg cell. Then we are each "knit together" as our heart and brain and arms and legs and stuff are shaped according to the plan God put there in the beginning.

Dad: Nicely put, Debbie.

The way a baby develops before birth makes me think of the way God created the earth and the universe!

Dad: How do you figure that?

When God created the earth He had a plan in His mind. He took stuff that was "without form," just like our unformed bodies, the egg cell, and put the parts together according to His plan.

Dad: I like that idea, Debbie. Instead of seeing evolution when we look at life before birth, we are really reminded of God's creation. "And God saw all that He had made, and, behold, it was very good."

Chapter 4

Beginning at the Beginning

We've talked a lot about YOU, and your life before birth. But what about your parents? How do your mother and father fit into the story of your life and your beginning?

The Bible has a lot to say about mothers and fathers and families, and so does biology. The family is one of God's greatest gifts. And it all began with God, for "God is love" (I John 4:8).

Our son, David, was asking us about those things.

All the stuff about how each of us developed inside Mom is great, Dad. But where do you fit in? I'm YOUR son, too, not just Mom's. What does the FATHER have to do with how the baby develops?

Dad: I was there right at your beginning.

But you said I started as a little round ball, the egg cell, inside Mom.

Dad: That's right. But it took *two* cells to form your first cell. One was the egg cell from your mother; one was the sperm cell from me.

I thought there had to be some reason I looked like both you and Mom.

Dad: You see, Dave, each cell in your body has 46 chromosomes; 23 came from your mother, and 23 came from me.

Chromosomes. Are those the things made out of DNA that tell our bodies how to grow and what to look like?

Dad: Close enough, Dave. A set of my chromosomes—my part of God's plan for making you—was packed into the head of a sperm cell. A sperm cell is really a very tiny cell, shaped sort of like a tadpole.

Mom: By the way, David, there are two kinds of sperm cells. One contains an "X" chromosome, and the other a "Y." A mother's egg cells are only one kind: "X."

Dad: So, when an "X" sperm joins an "X" egg, the baby is an "XX" girl, like your sisters. In your case, it was my "Y" sperm that joined Mom's "X," so your first cell began with an "XY" chromosome pair—and that's why you're a boy.

That's neat. I guess that shows God had everything planned ahead of time! But how do egg and sperm cells get together in the first place?

Mom: The story began a long time ago, David, when your father and I first met in high school. Over the next few years we did things together, talked a lot, and really got to know one another.

Dad: Finally, when I knew we loved one another and loved God enough to last a lifetime—through good times and bad—I asked your mom to marry me.

Mom: We knew we were ready to marry, too, Dave, because we wanted God to give us children. We knew children would take a lot of time and hard work, and need all the love we could give, but we could share with children the joy of living for Christ.

Dad: God provides a special way for husband and wife to have children in marriage. When your mom and I wanted to have you, our bodies joined together. It was like we had just one body or "one flesh."

Is that what the Bible means when it says a husband and wife "become one flesh"?

Mom: That's it exactly, David. But it was more than just our bodies. Our hearts and minds and spirits were one, too. As one body and spirit, we wanted to share our lives so that your life might begin.

Dad: Always remember this, too, son, God gives the special pleasure and rich joy of "becoming one" only to a husband and wife. God designed that very special kind of love to bind a husband and wife together in a deep-down happiness and devotion to each other, to their family, and to Him.

Wow! It sounds like God went to a lot of trouble just to make sure I was born! It was God's love and your love that made ME!

7

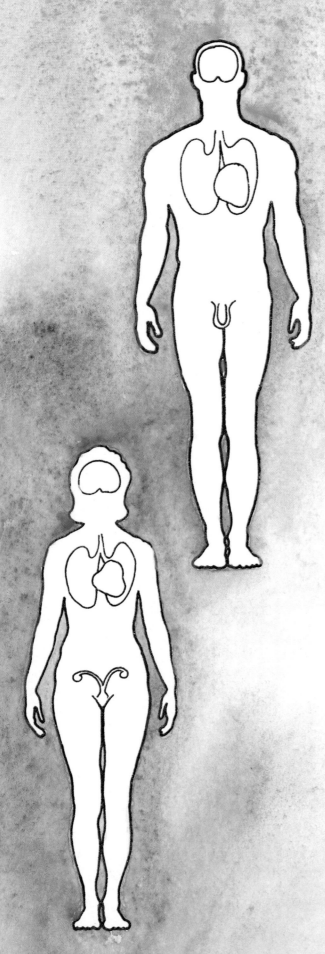

Mom: God was planning your birth even before he created Adam and Eve.

Dad: That's right, son. He created the first man and woman with wonderful bodies that had many similar parts. They both had brains, lungs, hearts, and other organs that work the same way. But in His perfect plan He gave them different organs for reproduction.

How are they different?

Dad: A man's reproductive organs are designed to make sperm cells and are on the outside of his body.

Mom: God placed a woman's reproductive organs on the inside of her body where the egg cells are made. This way her body can protect the baby and keep it safe as it grows and develops.

Dad: God designed the reproductive organs to fit together. One of my sperm cells joined with your mom's egg cell, and together they formed YOU—the first cell of your body.

I think I understand. After your two bodies became one, the sperm and egg cells became one, and that one was me!

Mom: That's right, and you began to grow inside my womb (*woom*). The womb, or uterus (*u′ ter us*), is the special place God designed for a baby to grow.

Dad: After nine months, when the baby is ready to be born, it travels from the womb to the outside through the birth canal.

Boy, God sure had to plan ahead to make sure everything worked right.

72

Mom: That just shows how special you are to God. God had you and your sisters in mind when your father and I grew to know each other, fell in love, married, and finally in marriage "became one."

Dad: When the egg and sperm cells join together, it's called *conception (con sep' shun).*

A lot of times the Bible says a certain woman "conceived and bore" a son or daughter. Does "conceived" mean conception, when the egg and sperm cells first get together?

Dad: That's right, David. The Bible and biology strongly agree on this point: your life begins at conception. That's when you became a special, unique, individual human being.

Mom: Of course, God had already planned for your life in eternity. But your biological life as a human being began at conception.

That sounds good to me, Mom. But I've heard people say an unborn baby is just part of the mother's body, and its okay if she wants to get rid of "it."

Dad: People say that because they want to make it easier for women to have abortions. But science clearly shows that it's *false* to call an embryo—or unborn baby—part of the mother's body.

Why do you say that, Dad?

Dad: You have wavy hair, your mother's hair is straight. You have one blood type, your mother has another. And, of course, you're a boy, your mother is a girl! All these differences—and all these things that make YOU—were written out in the DNA in your first cell. You were very different from *every cell* in your mother's body right from conception onward!

Does the Bible say that a baby is a special person, not just a part of his or her mother's body?

Mom: In the Bible God called Jacob and Esau and John the Baptist and Jesus by name before they were born. He even called Jeremiah to a special work before his birth (Jeremiah 1:5)! And remember, He knit together David, the psalm writer, as a special person inside his mother, just as He knit you together inside of me.

Dad: Finally, about nine months after God's plan for your life began to take shape, you were ready to be born.

Mom: And I was ready to give birth!

Being born must really be something. How does it happen? How did I get from the inside to the outside?

Mom: It took a lot of work (called labor), that's for sure! But the muscles in my womb and birth canal were designed to push and to stretch so you could be born—like you see in these pictures.

Did it hurt, Mom?

Mom: Yes it did, but only for a little while. And you were worth it!

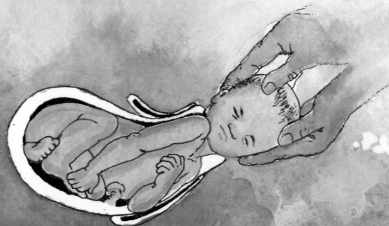

Dad: You had some work to do, too. Dave—especially breathing on your own for the first time.

Is that why the doctor spanks the baby, to start the baby breathing?

Dad: Sometimes a doctor does that, but the baby probably would start breathing anyway. It's important to clear the fluid out of the baby's throat and airway. Your heart and blood flow had to make some drastic changes at birth, too. But you were so well designed and planned ahead of time that these changes took place automatically in just a couple of minutes.

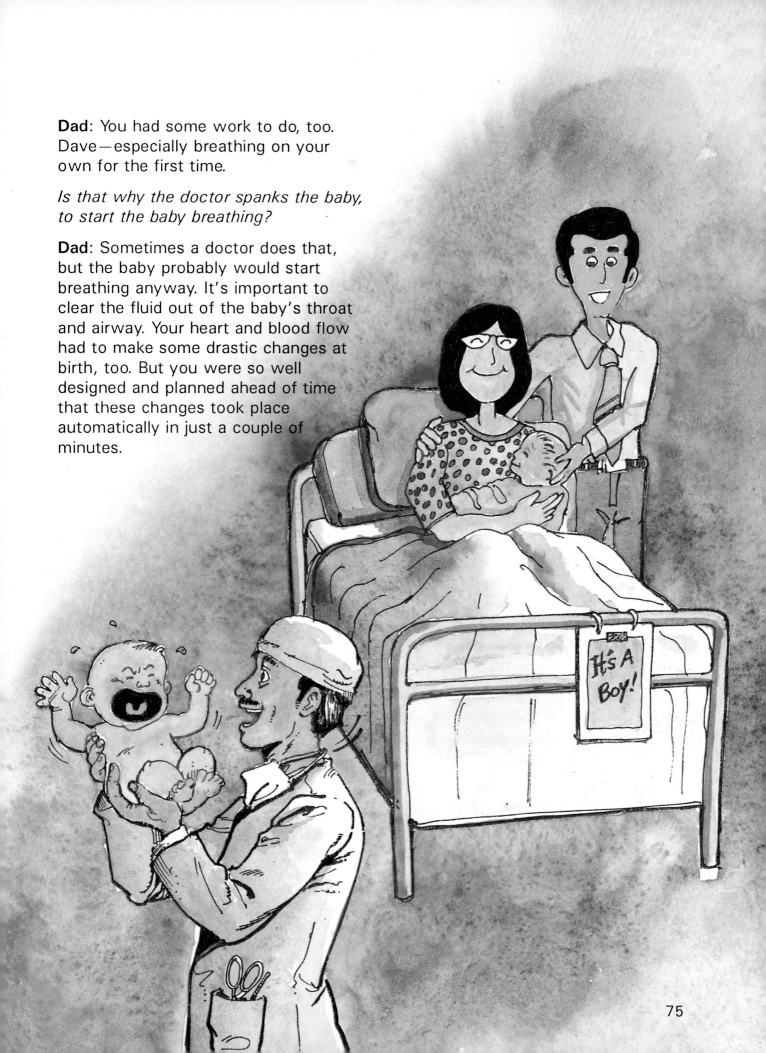

It's A Boy!

Mom: And there you were, our brand new baby boy!

But I wasn't really brand new, was I? By the time you saw me, I was already nine months old!

Dad: The Chinese call a baby one year old when it's born because it has almost finished its first year. It's more accurate according to both the Bible and biology (although nine months would be more accurate).

I have another question, Dad. It's kind of sad.

Dad: What is it, Dave?

What about the babies that don't come out right? Like you told Debbie, some children are born with a hole in the neck. Some are born with a lip and mouth not grown all the way together. I've seen pictures of babies born with hardly any arms and legs. If God planned us ahead of time, why do things like that happen?

Dad: Some birth defects are caused by drugs or other things the mother takes. But most birth defects are caused by mistakes in the DNA code. Scientists call those mistakes "mutations" (*mew tay' shuns*).

Mutations. I heard that mutations are supposed to make evolution happen. But really they just make birth defects and things like that. Is that right, Dad?

Dad: Yes it is. Like a tornado destroys a house or like rust ruins a car, mutations can make a mess of the beauty and function of God's perfect plan for the human body.

I've heard that sometimes a doctor can tell if a baby will be crippled or retarded or have a disease even before the baby is born. Are things like that sometimes caused by mutations?

Dad: Yes. And some people say the mother should have an abortion if she knows the baby has a problem before birth. What do you think, Dave?

I don't think anyone should ever have an abortion! After all, it isn't the little baby's fault that something is wrong. If I had a bicycle accident and got crippled, you wouldn't kill me and throw me away, would you?

Dad: Of course not, Dave! We love you because you're YOU, just the way God made you, with your own special purpose in His plan.

So, if I had an accident before birth, you would still keep me and love me, just the way you would if I had an accident after birth, right?

Mom: That's right. There's another reason the subject of abortion is so important. The courts are allowing people to kill babies before they are born because they are inconvenient or they don't meet certain standards. In time, there may be people who will want to kill others **after** they are born, just because they are sick, crippled, or very old.

Dad: Think about the great musical genius, Beethoven. His father and mother both had serious diseases that could affect their children, and they already had children who were deaf and blind. Beethoven did go deaf himself—but he wrote some of the greatest music the world has ever heard *after* he became deaf!

Boy, I guess that shows us that every life God gives is worth living!

Mom: We agree with you on that, Dave. But we must remember not every life that begins with problems ends up like Beethoven's. Sometimes babies are born who will never talk, or walk, or laugh, or see, or hear. Such babies often take a lot of time and money and special care, and they may put a strain on the whole family.

I know, Mom. But my friend had a baby brother that was born deformed, and it seems like their love for him draws the family closer together.

Dad: That's the way it should be. But some people find it hard to love a handicapped child, even harder still to love a little child before birth, a person they haven't even seen.

78

But that doesn't make the little tiny baby any less a person! Life is really a very special gift from God—problems or not. I think the very least we can do is help to make the most of the life God has given us.

Dad: That's right. The Apostle Paul doesn't deny that life may be full of hardships and suffering—but he also tells us that all the pain and trouble in our short life on earth is not even worth comparing to the great and glorious joy we'll have forever in heaven with Jesus (Romans 8:18)!

I think that's what I like best about being a Christian, Dad—knowing that God has a plan and purpose for me, no matter what happens.

Dad: I like that, too, Dave. And that means that even when bad things happen to us—even if those things happen before we were born—God can make all those bad things turn out for our good (Romans 8:28)!

Mom: Some people find it hard to believe that God loves them if they have a baby born with birth defects. They wonder how God could let this happen.

What's the answer?

Dad: The answer is easy to give, David—but *very hard* to accept. The answer is sin.

Mom: Remember I told you I had a lot of pain when you were born? Well, God didn't design my body that way when He made our first parents, Adam and Eve. But Adam and Eve sinned against God. They acted like God didn't love them. They even tried to put themselves in God's place. So God punished them. One of the ways He punished them was that the woman would experience pain in having children.

Dad: God's punishment for sin went even further than that. The whole universe began to fall apart, to grow old, to die—all when our first parents sinned. When God first created the world, He called it all "very good." There were no accidents, no mutations, no struggle, no death, and no birth defects.

Did sin change all that and mess up God's perfect world?

Mom: Yes, that's what the Apostle Paul tells us in Romans 8:20–21. The world was made subject to time and chance and brought under a bondage of decay or corruption because of sin.

Why did God have to punish sin so hard? Death, disease, and birth defects are really awful punishments.

Dad: Remember this, Dave. The penalty for sin *is* awful—but God paid that awful price Himself. Jesus Christ, God's only Son, suffered pain and death for us, so we could live again with God.

I know that with my mind, Dad. But it's hard to understand with my heart. I know Jesus paid the price for our sin with His pain and death. But why do we still have pain and death and birth defects?

Mom: Because God is not finished with us yet. Think about that new house being built down the street. Right now the roof has no shingles, the windows have no glass, and the sink has no water. Wouldn't you say that house is an awful mess?

Not really. That's the way a house is supposed to look at that stage. It's just not finished.

Dad: Do you remember the story in the Bible of the man born blind (John 9)? Jesus tells us that he was born blind so that, when Jesus healed him, others could see the power and love of God.

So I guess that man's blindness was part of God's plan for him, wasn't it?

Dad: Exactly. And remember this, too, Dave: when His disciples asked Him, Jesus said very directly that it was *not* that's man's sin, and it was *not* his parents' sin, that caused his blindness.

Mom: We have disease, birth defects, and death in our world because of sin in general. But just because a person has a defect or disease does NOT necessarily mean they are a bigger sinner than anyone else. In fact, the disease or defect they have may have a very special purpose in God's plan.

I understand, but I still feel sorry for the man born blind. The Bible says he was 40 years old when Jesus healed him.

Mom: I'm glad you feel sympathy for people who are hurting, Dave. The Bible says we will have trouble and tears in this world, and we do need to comfort one another.

Dad: But the trouble and tears are just for a short time, David. Then comes eternity (Romans 8:18), when God shall wipe away every tear, and death will be no more (Isaiah 25:8)!

I guess that's when God REALLY healed the man born blind—when He took him to heaven to live in paradise forever!

Dad: Right you are. God's "building plan" for us begins to take shape when egg and sperm make our first cell. His plan continues as we are born and grow up. But God's plan for us is not fully complete until we are reborn with perfect bodies in heaven!

It's so great to know that God has a perfect plan for each of us, and that He always knows what's best. Being born is wonderful. But being BORN AGAIN into God's eternal family is even more wonderful!

Leading Children to Jesus Christ

During the late elementary years boys and girls are open to a relationship with God. It is interesting that at this time in their lives they are able to understand the significance of making a commitment to the Lord.

Here are a few steps you can share that the Spirit can use to lead a child to Christ.

1. God loves you and wants you to become a member of His family. (I John 4:7–10)

2. Sin prevents you from being a member of God's family. Everyone has sinned. (Romans 3:23)

3. There is punishment for sin. Because everyone sins, everyone will receive this punishment. (Romans 6:23)

4. Jesus loves you so much that He died on the cross to take the punishment for your sins. (II Corinthians 5:21; I Peter 2:24)

5. If you want to receive the gift of Jesus' love, you must tell God about your sins and ask Him to forgive those sins. (I John 1:9)

6. If you ask Jesus into your heart and accept His love and trust in Him, His death means you won't have to be punished for you sins. Instead, you will become a member of God's Family and will have life forever. (John 3:16)

7. You should tell God and others about His great gift of love to you, and the happiness it brings.. (Romans 10:9–10)

Share with the parents of the child who has made a decision. Remember: *This is the most important choice a child or adult will ever make*.

Scriptures Relating to Parents and Children

Children are Blessed by Jesus

Mark 10:13-16

And they brought young children to him, that he should touch them: and his disciples rebuked those that brought them.

But when Jesus saw it, he was much displeased, and said unto them, Suffer the little children to come unto me, and forbid them not: for of such is the kingdom of God.

Verily I say unto you, Whosoever shall not receive the kingdom of God as a little child, he shall not enter therein.

And he took them up in his arms, put his hands upon them, and blessed them.

God's Promises

Proverbs 3:1-8

My son, forget not my law; but let thine heart keep my commandments:

For length of days, and long life, and peace, shall they add to thee.

Let not mercy and truth forsake thee: bind them about thy neck; write them upon the table of thine heart:

So shalt thou find favour and good understanding in the sight of God and man.

Trust in the LORD with all thine heart; and lean not unto thine own understanding.

In all thy ways acknowledge him, and he shall direct thy paths.

Be not wise in thine own eyes: fear the LORD, and depart from evil.

It shall be health to thy navel, and marrow to thy bones.

Proverbs 8:17

I love them that love me; and those that seek me early shall find me.

Proverbs 8:32

Now therefore hearken unto me, O ye children: for blessed are they that keep my ways.

Proverbs 23:15

My son, if thine heart be wise, my heart shall rejoice, even mine.

Isaiah 40:11

He shall feed his flock like a shepherd: he shall gather the lambs with his arm, and carry them in his bosom, and shall gently lead those that are with young.

Isaiah 54:13

And all thy children shall be taught of the LORD; and great shall be the peace of thy children.

Matthew 18:4-5

Whosoever therefore shall humble himself as this little child, the same is greatest in the kingdom of heaven.

And whoso shall receive one such little child in my name receiveth me.

Matthew 18:10

Take heed that ye despise not one of these little ones; for I say unto you, that in heaven their angels do always behold the face of my Father which is in heaven.

Matthew 19:14

But Jesus said, Suffer little children, and forbid them not, to come unto me: for of such is the kingdom of heaven.

Luke 9:48

And said unto them, Whosoever shall receive this child in my name receiveth me: and whosoever shall receive me receiveth him that sent me: for he that is least among you all, the same shall be great.

Commandments to Children

Exodus 20:12

Honour thy father and thy mother: that thy days may be long upon the land which the LORD thy God giveth thee.

Proverbs 6:20–23

My son, keep thy father's commandment, and forsake not the law of thy mother:

Bind them continually upon thine heart, and tie them about thy neck.

When thou goest, it shall lead thee; when thou sleepest, it shall keep thee; and when thou awakest, it shall talk with thee.

For the commandment is a lamp; and the law is light; and reproofs of instruction are the way of life.

Ephesians 6:1

Children, obey your parents in the Lord: for this is right.

2 Timothy 2:22

Flee also youthful lusts: but follow righteousness, faith, charity, peace, with them that call on the Lord out of a pure heart.

Children are a Gift from God

Genesis 4:1

And Adam knew Eve his wife; and she conceived, and bare Cain, and said, I have gotten a man from the LORD.

Genesis 17:16

And I will bless her, and give thee a son also of her: yea, I will bless her, and she shall be a mother of nations; kings of people shall be of her.

Psalms 127:3

Lo, children are an heritage of the LORD: and the fruit of the womb is his reward.

Proverbs 17:6

Children's children are the crown of old men; and the glory of children are their fathers.

Have a Teachable Spirit

Colossians 3:20

Children, obey your parents in all things: for this is well pleasing unto the Lord.

Matthew 18:4

Whosoever therefore shall humble himself as this little child, the same is greatest in the kingdom of heaven.

Proverbs 13:1

A wise son heareth his father's instruction: but a scorner heareth not rebuke.